Sitting in the Sky

Annie Deppe

SUMMER PALACE PRESS

First published in 2003 by

Summer Palace Press
Cladnageeragh, Kilbeg, Kilcar, County Donegal, Ireland

Printed by Nicholson & Bass Ltd.

A catalogue record for this book is available
from the British Library

ISBN 0 9544752 0 8

This book is printed on elemental chlorine-free paper

for Theo,
and for Caitlin, Peter and Michael

Acknowledgments

Versions of some of the poems in this book have appeared in: *The Recorder*, *THE SHOp*, and *The Stinging Fly*.

Biographical Note
Annie Deppe was born in Hartford, Connecticut. She is a dual citizen of Ireland and the United States. In 2000 she and her husband moved to Cape Clear Island, West Cork. They have also lived in Mín a' Leá, County Donegal. She was awarded a B.A. in English from Earlham College and an M.A. in Educational Psychology from the University of Connecticut. In 2002 she received an M.A. in Creative Writing from Poets' House / Lancaster University and was chosen by Poetry Ireland to read in their Introductions Series.

CONTENTS

Innocence

What did Laura and I know? We were kids
playing in the barn. It was always
the verge of night in that two-storey maze.

Where the old Victrola came from, I'll
never know. A gift from the past. Almost
as tall as we were, it resembled a little mahogany

townhouse with a lid like a mansard roof.
Tiny doors opened and shut to adjust
the sound. No needle, so we snapped

inch-long thorns from a Japanese quince,
fitted them to the arm and played
the 78 record we found. Billie Holiday.

Under the thorn her voice was low as a man's
and scratchy. Long ago, a hired hand
killed himself in that barn and sometimes,

as the Victrola wound down, we wondered
if Billie's quince-distorted voice was his.
We took turns winding the crank, playing

the record over and over, music
different from any we'd heard before.
I don't mean just rough from thorns.

These songs ignited and burned. Sparked
something we knew our parents wouldn't like.
We couldn't get enough.

If my man ain't got no money
And I say 'take all mine, honey'
Ain't nobody's business if I do.

One day my father caught us
dancing to Billie with our shirts off.
Laura was sent straight home

and the Victrola, our house-of-spirits,
disappeared. Not so easy, Daddy,
to take away the pull of a song.

Tonight those words come back
as I drive through storm-shadowed mountains.
I'm singing Billie Holiday, realize

I'm picturing Laura as she danced that day:
shoulders bare, just a hint of breasts,
how she assumed a pose of world-

weariness, tried heartbreak on for size.
As if any of us ever needed to go looking
for heartbreak. As I sing, it's not Billie

I'm imitating, but Laura imitating Billie.
A squall of hail. I pull the car to the shoulder,
let the winds rock me, listen to the voice of ice.

Brasstown, 1969

It was June and in those blue-smoked hills
of North Carolina we thought ourselves at war

with our country. As planes napalmed
Vietnam, we worked tomato fields, suckering

leggy plants through sweltering afternoons,
wrapping tendrils around coarse twine.

We called ourselves the Brasstown Six.
After my first year of college I took a summer job

so I wouldn't have to go home. What did I
know of growing tomatoes? I'd spent years

trying not to be alone with my father
in his garden. Tomatoes were an experiment:

six of us imported from around the country
to try a cash crop other than tobacco.

The plants stained our hands the same colour
as the slow green creek. Copperheads everywhere

yet we walked at night through high grasses
barefoot. We believed, somehow, we'd smell

the snakes. Susie from Chicago stashed
her pot in the furniture-filled chicken coop.

By the end of July, the Brasstown Six
would be down to five; before summer's end,

we'd all be gone. One night at a bar in Murphy
we watched as Neil Armstrong stepped

down to the Sea of Tranquility. Next day, Susie
weeded topless: *one giant step for womankind.*

A letter for Rick. Selective Service
ordering him to report. For most of that night

we sat on the porch of the farmhouse,
gazed over fields pulsing with fireflies,

argued how to keep Rick out of the army
and failed. He climbed the steps of the Greyhound bus

and was lost to us. Before we let him go
we circled his hickory-split chair on the porch.

Morning mists hung in the valley
as we passed around scissors. Still urging him

towards Canada, we clipped
his long brown strands, wanting to cheat

the army, at least, of this small victory.
In the weedy fields that day,

rotting fruit already filled our nostrils.
I've never known what happened to Rick.

Only had one last visit when he found me
at my Quaker college and slouched

on the dormitory couch in green fatigues.
He couldn't speak about the future, so we talked

of tomatoes and fireflies, whole fields of fireflies
which once moved beneath us.

Samhain, Cape Clear Island

We want our letters to go out
on tomorrow morning's ferry,
so we carry them to the post office
on Paddy Leonard's farm.

We head then to the abandoned lighthouse.
We'll need to walk fast to get back
before dark. The cusp of seasons, wind
colder than it's been all fall.

Barely pausing to touch the tower,
we turn and start home,
greet kerchiefed Eleanor
who's planting daffodils with a pickaxe.

At our neighbours', a tractor
and cattle wagon left at the lane's end
block our way. Edging round
the machinery, we're startled

by a swirl of music
though there's not a soul in sight.
It's the wind weaving broken scales
through the wagon's metal bars.

Years ago, before my father died,
my mother opened a window
in their bedroom, raised
the panes enough to slip in place

a slender, wooden, slotted box.
That instrument through which wind
might speak never really worked –
not enough breath to raise a tune.

Even so, I'm surprised
that years later, when it was time
to clear the house, my sister and I
threw out that wind harp.

These days, I wear an antique ring
from Mother's great-aunt, a woman
vain as a summer day.
She had the gift to see

the unseeable. For her,
it was a kind of game.
But one night, as a young wife,
something happened

in her marriage bed
that scared her so much
she closed tight those inner eyes.
Never spoke of what she saw.

Once, I went with two friends
to meet a man who could photograph
the soul. I still wonder why
the pictures all were black-and-white.

As we left, he said, *Loved ones*
who've passed over are standing
at the sides of two of you. No one dared
ask which of us stood alone.

My Mother Speaks of Elizabeth Bishop

At first I knew her only as 'that quiet girl'. This was Vassar
back in '32, and already she was rumoured to write poems.
She sat behind me at convocation where she tapped
her foot against my chair as Edna St. Vincent Millay

read, no, declaimed her verses. Next evening,
she knocked at my tower-room door. *What did you
think of Edna St. Cheesecake Millay?* I lit the silver chafing-dish,
let blue spirit flames heat Welsh rarebit.

A moth beat against my lampshade as we dismantled
the new Baudelaire translations. Later, we climbed the metal ladder
to the slant rooftop. Bish leaned against the chimney and smoked,

pointed out the Seven Sisters. Writing, it seemed, might be our lives.
But Annie, you should have seen me up there, gazing out
over the edge, bracing my feet against those iron Victorian rails.

The Card Players

In the depths of the Depression
a young woman fresh from Vassar
slid down from a mule in Hindman, Kentucky,
her leather satchel filled with poetry,
and each word she heard

stretched at least a syllable longer
than when she boarded the train
in Philadelphia. She met her new pupils
in the heart of America
and found she couldn't understand a word.

Four years he courted her, driving
his black Model A back and forth
from Connecticut to Kentucky.
Is it true that when they were engaged,
my father made my mother

memorize the name of the brook
which ran through his land?
Naromi-yock-now-hu-sunk-a-tank-shunk.
As children we learned to rattle it off.
What test did my mother set him in return?

Three days of rain when I was five.
Overnight, the waters rose. I dreamed
my parents were fighting again –
why do I always remember them fighting
when so many evenings they walked

arm-in-arm the boundaries of our land?
This time it wasn't harsh words that woke me
but the roar of water. Without warning,
we found ourselves cut off
as our brook swelled and fields turned to lakes.

Wanting to view disaster close up,
we inched down the mud path, clung
to branches, gazed at the deluge that trapped
our family. I can still feel
my mother's hand clutching the back of my slicker.

That night, by lamplight, nobody going
anywhere, we sat around the table
for game after game of cards – dirty hearts –
the transistor radio turned up loud,
broadcasting names of flooding rivers,

making a certain music from misfortune:
the Connecticut, the Housatonic,
the Quinebaug, the Willimantic.
Father shuffling the deck like a child,
Mother on one of her lucky streaks.

Maybe she'll never write another poem,
but at each game's end, she's holding
the Jack of Diamonds. No one wants
to sit on her left – even to kids she'll unload
the Queen of Spades, without mercy.

The Minister's Wife

Mother squints along the rifle's length,
one eye closed, takes aim,
the butt tucked into her shoulder so snugly
that fifty years later I can feel the kick.
She's in the field near the garden. Striped
apron pulled tight around her waist.
Hair pinned back – she always wore it back.

Behind her, my two brothers sit in the long grass,
their eyes fixed on her. Or on the gun. Their mouths
form nearly identical o's. Where they twirl
hay between their fingers, the photo blurs.
Why is this the one picture I stole
from the album in the attic? My mother takes sight
and aims at something I'll never see.

Stars and Stones

We circled the stainless steel trolley,
a minister's family not quite able to remember
the 23rd Psalm. Your bun unpinned,
hair fanned out, eyes and mouth
almost closed. We emerged

from the funeral home into April snow,
the roads treacherous all the way back
to your house where we ate toast by the kitchen fire,
sat up late telling stories. When we retired
with our spouses into skinny,

childhood beds, no one slept in yours.
And the wind. Such a wind that night.
Snow lashed the windows and
the weeping willow snapped
under the storm's white weight.

Before my father died,
the two of you worked out a signal –
Watch for me. If the bedroom door opens
and you see no one there, it's me
come to let you know there is another side.

You waited. The door remained shut.
Too keyed up for sleep the night you died,
Theo and I just lay there, arms around each other,
when – with a resounding
crack – our bedroom door flew open.

All this comes back when Theo says
Let's see who's out here.
He means what constellations
he's learned under island skies. I try to make out
not the shapes of Greeks

but the faces of my dead.
When my father died, I walked our dog
under winter stars, knew those points of light
weren't heaven, yet wondered in what crack
of the universe a dead father might still live.

Now layer on layer of wind off water
rises in the dark. Each tier
with its own pitch and speed.
My husband loves such nights,
calls wind the breath of life.

I hate the wind. It tangles my hair,
makes my head ache. After the funeral,
we returned to find a host of snow geese,
back-lit and golden, scavenging
in stubble behind your house.

I collect dreams of you, Mother.
Gather them like stones
to mark each visit. Little gifts
from your world. From that mound,
these three dreams:

you show up towards dawn
in the Volkswagen camper
you always wanted – levitate
outside the bedroom window,
then streak away into amber clouds.

And then you're back again,
this time in an evergreen Ford Explorer.
You're getting ready for the Grand Tour,
wonder if I'd like to come along.
And last night: at a church supper

I ask you where you'd like to sit.
You gesture towards a table. *Why
with my friends, of course.*
We join the ladies for the meal.
All of them lively, none of them breathing.

Night Singing

As they readied to leave, my father
reached into his suit-coat pocket, brought out
a handful of coins. *You might want to play a few songs.*

I lined up ten shiny dimes on the cotton sheet.
Above me, a radio mounted on the wall.
I was five, could count to over one hundred.

In the corner bed, a boy named Jimmy wailed.
Only four. *Cry baby.* This was before
they wheeled me into the dark brown room

and the bad mask clamped down over my nose.
Before backwards counting. That night
I lay waiting in the hospital's half-light,

slid one thin dime after another into the radio's slot.
The row grew shorter, and it suddenly
came to me – if I used the last coin

they would never come back.
Of my mother, all I remembered
was her hair folded in a bun, and of my father,

his speckled white hands. As I fell asleep
I heard them singing on radio, trying
to comfort me. A hundred miles away.

Still Life with Storm

Rage off to take my shower. Find I've forgotten
the spider that lives above the tub. In our house
you're the one who catches spiders and mice,
carries them to that place beyond the wall.
You're the one who gets all jobs involving death and insects.

How then, when you've scooped it into a cup
and dumped it outside, can there be a spider in the exact
same place each day? After I push my way past you
determined to claim first shower, after my nightgown
lies bunched on the bathroom floor, I know suddenly

what waits behind the plastic curtain. I pull on my nightclothes
not wanting to show my nakedness, then cry for help.
I never understood how, in the lust of battle, armies could pause
for a holiday, but you place our fight on hold, walk that spider out
to where the gentlest of rains, you say, has begun to fall.

The Slap

The sweltering day we buried my grandmother
I scored a pink padded bra. Strange to recall how,

back then, pink was considered daring.
I was Midwestern, seventeen, and my parents –

finalizing funeral plans – must have been
out of their minds to let me wander Newark alone,

the city still smouldering after summer riots,
burnt cars edging the streets.

I bought the bra in a kind of discount store
where gleaming black women

stacked garments with practised hands.
There was nowhere there to try it on, so

back in my grandmother's dark
upstairs apartment, I found the pink bra puffed

in a most unnatural way. Still, I yearned to feel
my boyfriend discover it beneath my dress.

In the humid church that afternoon, I bent to kiss
Grandma's cold brow and marvelled how in death

she seemed a little less stern. I touched her cheek
and recalled the slap she gave for letting the boys watch me

wash our family car. If I loved her, I also loved
that two-piece bathing suit. Behind me, mourners

murmured as I straightened and pushed up my bra strap,
raw scent of gladioli pulsing through the church.

In Residence, 107 Water Street

Our first night in James Merrill's brass bed
you ask, between kisses, if I am afraid.
A breeze blows in, scented with fresh-baked bread –
a gift from our host beyond the grave?

We never met Jimmy. Now our clothes
share closet space with his blue birkenstocks
(same size as mine), striped suspenders, silk bow-
ties and four Greek beach robes. But it's not

until 3 a.m. that, wide awake, I climb
the steep stairs to the black-and-white checkered floor,
sit at his weathered grand piano, find
sea air has cancelled half the notes. Whole scores

rise, though, in the wind beyond the star-deck.
Whose hands on mute keys could catch that music?

Moorings

1

Almost November, the sky a thickening grey.
One silver-gold ray escapes to burnish
this stretch of harbour. New to Stonington,

I've puzzled over a double-craft working
the waters these past few days – a small boat
pushing a platform. At the controls,

an old man or woman dressed in black watch cap,
blue sweatshirt, and orange rubber overalls.
This jerry-rigged contraption motors

among the season's last pleasure boats.
Each day another sailboat's gone.
Calling from Cambridge just now, Molly says

they've been picking green beans and basil.
Still no killing frost. Out on the water, though,
it looks cold. The double boat slows and circles.

An orange buoy is winched like a flood victim
and dropped safely on deck.
Then I understand: it's time to pull the moorings.

Still talking to Molly, I wish she could see it all –
russet trees across the harbour, the return to port
of a red trawler, seagulls trailing above its wake,

and this buoy boat, the name *Lion Heart*
stencilled on her stern, working the moorings,
readying them for the winter to come.

2

Molly said yesterday she's always sad
this time of year. Too much loss.
Already she's turned on the bank of lights

she bought to help stave off this mood.
She eats her breakfast beneath an artificial sun.
Two Novembers back, as we prepared

to sell the family home, it was Molly
who encountered our father, dead a dozen years.
She moved aside for him on the winding stairs.

Confusion on his face as he held
the trembling tea tray, then turned and retreated
back down the steps. That evening he did not

take his dead wife her usual breakfast-in-bed.
I'm at my window again looking out
across rooftops to the harbour.

Two black birds alight on the house
opposite ours. One settles
on a chimney pot – for the view, or perhaps

for warmth? The other shelters
in the decorative brick zigzag just below.
I am tempted towards one last, October swim.

Maybe this afternoon. Sunstrikes meet water,
turn it white. A white so brilliant, so black,
I'm afraid I might get lost. It begins to snow.

3

I sat cross-legged on the living-room couch
talking with my dead mother. We were laughing.
Now, I carry the day's first coffee to the pier,

savour this fragment of last night's dream.
The dock's planking has been pulled up
for the season. Close by, the buoy boat works

a mooring, catches up the summer float and drops
a winter marker: odd wedge of Styrofoam angling up
in the water's wake like a cock-eyed slab of ice.

Wave-splash against the stone embankment
and there by the pier a jellyfish blossoms,
two feet across, in the same water

where I've let my feet dangle at night.
It's doing a dead-man's float. Crimson,
like an Asian water lily, with garish star-bursts

and tangles the colour of bruises or plum pulp.
One stringy tentacle seeks and finally
grasps the stony wall, takes anchor.

Churning water from the departing boat
flips the jellyfish over, exposing its shaggy
underside – scarlet, open – but it holds fast.

To-and-fro then until its body is ripped
away. That single gauzy strand, clinging
fiercely to the wall, continuing to wave.

When the World Becomes Water

Little one, the dark's not far off. Is this the night you'll lift
like the heron who circles the flood with easy wings,
then settles on long legs like the legs of our house?
My husband glides through rosewood trees, sets

monkeypots adrift from his canoe, then waits
while silvery seeds float above the invisible world.
If ember fish appear, he's ready with his bow.
Perhaps though, the dolphin-fish will tip him

into the watery realm and steal his shape.
If the dolphin-man steps beneath the palm leaves...
If the dolphin-man slips into my hammock,
the women say I'll know him when the room swirls

and night birds call *oh manioc, sweet manioc, wild
manioc and mangoes*. My long-legged traveller,
are you near? The black-and-red bird screams
and pink blossoms float upon the waters.

Fireworks, Hallowe'en

We returned to the island to find,
in the high field above the harbour,
Kerry cows where the horse once grazed.
Since then, Peter, when we've
called you in New York,

I've wondered what I'd say
if you asked about Peggy.
You spent hours last summer
coaxing that chestnut mare, luring
her across the field with a half-eaten apple,

offering her treats each day.
You've never spoken of her, though.
Only after we pressed our neighbours,
What happened to the horse? were we told,
Three men were crossing the field...

Tonight you'll parade the streets
of Greenwich Village. *The city
needs some fun again, and no one does Hallowe'en
like the Village.* I picture sinewy
lines of costumed revellers

dancing through night canyons
as jazz riffs clash with marimba, then spark
and merge to pulsate off concrete walls.
So much body heat
warming the city. You'll put on neon glasses

and a mix of cheap jewelry,
a blue wig barely able to cover
your waist-length chestnut hair –
a poor man's costume, you call it.
Later you'll stop in at a hat show,

whatever that may be. There's so much
about your life I can only guess at.
Beneath everything, your descriptions
of how, at the end of your street, smoke
still rises from ground zero.

When three men crossed that field
and Peggy spooked, she fled in terror, snagged
her leg in fence-wire and catapulted
– how do you pull those you love
back from the edge? – catapulted

down gorse and bracken,
shot past rocks and gulls to the harbour.
And when that flight exploded in water,
her leg still snared by wire,
and when those three men ran down the hill,

rowed out to where Peggy
still struggled, they slipped a rope
around her neck to save her,
only to have her thrash
and scream and finally drown.

Tonight, from a field above the harbour,
we watch fireworks rise from the mainland,
mute bursts of colour. Nearby, black shapes graze
where a horse ought to be.
In this shadowland, everything blends.

March

I step out to bring the clothes in off the line
and find the hill above our house on fire.

Black smoke, lashed with orange, billows
across the fields. We've seen gorse fires spread
on the mountains across the bay,

but these flames just beyond our stone wall
are a different matter. No fire station
on this island, so we're at the mercy –

at least it's a west wind blowing away from our house.
Heat flushes a pair of curlews from their nest.

–

In the burnt field above our home, curl
of snail shell seared white against the black.

Down at the harbour, the boats were blessed
this morning. Last week, smudge of ashes
to remind us nothing lasts. Years ago, in Mexico,

I took photos of yellow flowers hung on homes
to keep roofs safe from wind. Each evening
when the Angelus rings, I find my prayer list longer.

Three hooded crows circle the white-footed calf.
Back in New England, two feet of fresh snow

as our son leaves in the dark to drive to work.
I seem to have given up sleeping at night.

–

Bridge-fall in Portugal, train crash in England:
March, my birth month. Once as a surprise,
my husband had my star chart read for me.

For an hour an astrologer explained my life. Said
she'd never seen such a fractured chart.
That afternoon I took the long way home,

smaller and smaller country roads.
Wasn't in any hurry to see my husband and children.

Unwilling to surrender the illusion
of serenity, I hid the tape of that reading.

Haven't listened to it since. Haven't stopped listening.

Dún an Óir

Today the cows' backs are slick with mist.
Only the Fastnet's foghorn hints
at surrounding sea. We're climbing

the Leaca Mhór – Faith Hill, it's also called.
The road's pitched steep as a ladder.
Without a car it is an act of faith.

So many Sundays this hill convinces me to stay
at home with coffee, the house to myself.
I'm having trouble with faith these days.

First of April, the end of Lent,
and isolated primroses brighten the morning.
In the church, heaters on the walls glow red.

The wet sounds of Irish wash over me:
A Thiarna, déan trócaire, Lord have mercy,
one of the few parts I understand.

We arrived on this island with
two suitcases, a box of books,
and my threadworn bag of worries.

A friend says I need to hand over fear
but unless I can picture every disaster
how do I keep my loved ones safe?

The sun and the Calf Islands
are still lost in mist as we start home.
Coming over the rise there's a place

where most days you catch sight
of *Dún an Óir*, the Castle of Gold.
Today, though, only this fog

with its beaded spider webs
suspended from gorse, and its thrush
singing somewhere beyond the wall.

Good Friday, Cape Clear Island

Along the roadside, celandines
whip about in sunlight. Sound of a car
behind us as we walk the steep road out of Gleann.
We're ready to flatten ourselves into the hedgerow,
but it is minutes before the ancient
blue Volvo, which doubles as the island's hearse,
labours past, a flick of a wave
from the woman in the passenger seat.

Coming over the hill, we find we've caught up –
like being in a cortège so slow is the pace,
but this time the Volvo's back is empty.
We follow it towards the shell-pink church.
Roaringwater Bay opens out before us, fractures
into ten thousand colours we cannot name.

Walking Glen West

I couldn't say what longing
rose up in me as I climbed

the faint path towards the Bullig,
evening light hammering

the hillside golden. First
heather of the year, small bright globes

mixing with the gorse's thorny yellow
and the susurration

of long-stemmed grasses, purple,
flowing beside the path which keeps

rising above green harbour waters.
I found, as I followed dried cattle prints

and sought footholds on steep ledge faces,
something inside was pressing up.

Even before I reached the cliffs
at the island's shoulder with their early

summer spread of yellow trefoils,
sea pinks waving, even before

the skylark's song spiralled upwards,
something was making itself felt:

watching the long waves sweep in
I realized my father has come

and wrapped himself around this island.
So many years since his death.

So many years since I threw earth
into his grave and willed him to stay

buried. While I sat high above the sea
and watched, far out, a red boat rock,

while I sat near the graves
of drowned sailors, their heads and feet

marked by field stones, buried in sight
of where they washed ashore,

I realized I've reached the age
my father was the summer he spent

drowning. I was six, he took me out to fish
as he foundered in his own dark waters,

could not find the air he needed.
This morning, when I saw pink-grey fish

in North Harbour, I recalled how he'd rent a boat
and row to the end of Roseland Lake

where we'd drift on weedy waters
and pull pumpkin fish, one flat orange body

after another, and then, too bony to eat,
throw them back again. All about our boat –

am I remembering this right? –
little dead suns with unthinking eyes.

One steamy August afternoon,
we children were sent to wait

on the back-porch swing while the doctor came
and stole our real father away.

I wish in some ways he'd died that day,
spared us those years of fear and anger.

If you make your father mad, you will kill him.
When Daddy's raging face loomed

above me, I turned and ran.
It took him thirty years to die.

Waves gather and hurdle over jagged
rocks half-submerged beneath the sea.

Up here, the rough yellow light
of curled lichen threads. What surprises me

after all this time is that something in me
is softening. Recently, I'm remembering

curling up in his lap, and how
his hearing aid – the old one

clipped to the top of his undershirt –
squealed and made us laugh.

How he'd cut an apple in half, show me
the star of Bethlehem hidden within.

Late sun slides into cloud banks
above the mainland's mountains,

black-backed gulls ride currents
and swallows dip and swoop. Once

I watched fireworks with my parents
by the Quinebaug River. Chrysanthemums

filled the air, but my youngest son,
frightened by the noise, began to cry.

His grandfather, so often
lacking patience, lifted him onto his lap,

tucked Michael's head beneath
his jacket flap to muffle the sound.

How is it that anger and love can be
wrapped so tightly against our hearts?

Held close like that
against his grandfather's chest,

a place of warmth and darkness,
Michael calmed, then burrowed part way out

until, ears still sheltered, he could peer up
into the coloured night.

I must have once been held
that way myself. My father must have been

a tent, spread out against the sky.

Winter

Sometimes, when someone tells a ghost story,
my husband pours me another glass of wine, says
Why don't you tell them about the plane? I often find
I unwind that thirty-year-old memory

as if it were a fairy tale, the girl walking into the woods
with her father in search of a lost family. In those days
the girl preferred never to walk in the woods with her father,
but the family had been dead

almost a week when the man rose up
and came to her in that space we sometimes inhabit
between waking and sleep. Already dead, what force
could launch him through woods and stubbled cornfields

to a line he somehow couldn't cross?
Later, when she called it a dream, she knew it wasn't.
His motion was slow, stretched against natural law,
until he stood in December grass and called for help.

A silent call which reached the farmhouse's back bedroom
so next morning the girl and her father set off to search.
Pockets filled with candy, they entered the woods,
guessing at each new turn – no, not guessing,

for miles they were almost led
through a maze of logging roads and deer trails.
Why tell this like a fairy tale?
Why can't I say what happened?

Above my father and me, fresh white branch breaks,
and when we turned together we saw, over the stone wall,
lime-green pieces of a plane
scattered across forest floor. The family had been dead

almost a week when my father crossed to them
and, the dance not yet done, at the same moment
we gazed into the treetop and saw the boy cradled there.
Before dark and the winter's first snow,

chain-saws brought the boy to earth.
If sometimes I tell this like a fairy tale, maybe it's because
at the heart of such stories is horror.
And yet, strangely, it seems now

one of my best days with my father,
not afraid of him as together we headed home.
Where the path narrowed, he walked ahead
and seemed older, human, his boots worn on one side.

The Bullig Path

Tired from packing, we walk to the cliffs
behind our house, not wanting to leave
this island home. I settle in the rock chair,

my favourite place to watch for whales,
while you and Cait hike the steep path
down to the sea arch. The blue of your shirt

and her red skirt grow smaller and smaller,
then vanish over the edge.
I adjust the binoculars – no whales,

just broken lines of gannets.
Off the Bullig, where Atlantic waters curl
and crash, the head of a seal surfaces;

then with a roll, its slick body slides from sight.
So strange how you can be in my view
one moment, then suddenly gone.

There are nights when I wake and study
your face. You're the age my father was
the first time he died. I don't know how, love,

I'd ever be ready to let you go.
Some say the Bullig Path was worn into the earth
by generations wanting one last glimpse

as loved ones sailed from the island.
You're climbing back up the hill again, and not
for the first time I'm struck by the way our daughter

looks like my mother. For a moment, is
my mother, young again, striding along
at your side. Suddenly, nothing seems fixed

in a world where sea caves tunnel
beneath my feet, and my dead mother walks
at my husband's side. *It's the strangest thing,*

you say, as you reach me. *When I looked up
and saw you on the ridge,
you seemed to be sitting in the sky.*

Chinese Dragons in a Donegal Landscape

I can hear you humming that Tom Waits song,
the one we danced to half-way through supper.
You always put it on when you want us in bed together –
your idea of a good house-warming. Just back

from our first walk out the high bog road towards Errigal,
I want to sit now at my desk beneath the banner
of Chinese dragons. Let them swim twin circles
through clouds and chrysanthemums

as I write down how, in evening light, we mistook
white caps on the mountain lake for swans.
Outside, gales which threaten never to stop
batter the panes. It's started raining so hard

a small pool gathers on the inside window-ledge.
Slowly the sea shells you gave me last summer
become islands. Downstairs, love, you've moved on
to Diana Krall and turned the music up.

The Road from Mín a' Leá

Coasting downhill above
the fish farm, there's a moment
when great wings
lift from reeds, then glide
along glistening banks.
Not for us the lives of herons.

The Aghla mountains – those two
white horses – flank this valley.
Across the river, the red door
of an empty house gleams.
And in the distance
beyond Ballyness, light

breaks upon black waves.
Last night, I walked beneath pines
in whose branches a choir
of hooded crows slept.
Above us all, those drowned boys
in their tattered winter robes.

The Reader

So few cars come down this mountain road
    that when one makes a sharp stop
        in front of our house tonight, it's news.

We're at the window, afraid it's hit a sheep
    or spun off the road down the steep bank.
        Red tail-lights and the air fills with a mix

of motor and loud music. Dark buzz
    as two tall boys with slurred voices
        argue in the high beam. Above their heads

they raise flagstones from our wall,
    then heave them, two-handed, over the edge.
        You're pulling on your trousers,

filled with some male need to be out in the night
    facing this hyped-up energy head-on.
        As you move towards the door,

switching on lights, making your presence known,
    they're back in their car and gone.
        I wait in my nightgown as you search, twice,

the hillside with a flashlight. Wonder
    what I would have done this far up the glen
        had those boys turned their energies

towards our windows, or you. Next morning we find
    hidden by high grass
        the curled body of a badger:

eyes open, teeth bared, haloed by stones.
        Did those boys kill for fun? Or, once the car hit it
            did they stop to put it out of misery

in a drunken act of mercy?
        I put on the water for coffee and begin
            to make breakfast. You grab the newspaper,

start outside, then pause to read an article on Gustav Mahler
        before you scoop up the badger in those pages
            and try to walk death out of sight.

Camillo

From the guesthouse veranda I see a dog
sneak by, dragging a bleached, curved bone.
Later, the same dog, curled in a nest

of weeds in the old graveyard, a litter
clamped to her side. The dog's eyes
say too much about this world.

Alma wants me to meet Juanita and Camillo.
We pass makeshift shops with radishes
set out on boards, dingy video arcades,

until we come to a flight of stairs cut
into the steep hill. Here we descend
endlessly. Worn stone steps plummet

past cement-block houses. In a dusty yard,
a young girl surrounded by fallen red blossoms
talks earnestly to a green parakeet on her finger.

We reach what looks like an animal shed
built into a narrow toe-hold.
Then I spot the outdoor kitchen

where a woman stirs a large pot over a fire.
This is the home of Juanita and Camillo.
Above the door, someone has nailed

a cross fashioned from yellow flowers.
Because Camillo says he wants to see the sky,
neighbours help Juanita carry her husband's bed

out beneath the jacaranda tree. They smooth
his pink blanket and from a branch
drape plastic sheets, Camillo's canopy.

All night, at the guesthouse up the hill,
I listened to the sound of running water
as a young man tended plants.

Here everything is dry, but what
surprises me now is how gentle
the evening sun feels, and how

this tiny strip of dirt takes on the feel of a courtyard
with Camillo placed in the centre of everything:
neighbours coming and going,

leaving gifts of coins
tucked under his pillow, small boys
chasing cacophonous chickens, somebody

singing somewhere as Alma hangs
the I.V. bottle from a branch, yellow liquid drifting
through the plastic tube. For years, the couple

tended the graveyard where this morning
I saw the dog. They worked for nothing
but the promise of a plot someday.

That day may come soon, but for the moment,
on this small flat place, on the way down
the steep hill, Camillo is holding court.

Domatilla

Take a city famous for its greenness
and white mansions locked away behind tall walls.

It could be anywhere, but this time make it Mexico.
In the heart of this city, surrounding the *estación*

where all trains enter and leave,
place a second city of thirty thousand souls.

Say this day you get confused
as you leave the train station, get lost, find yourself

in a dead end. It feels like a dream gone wrong
except now an opening appears. Two girls,

legs dangling, sit on a wooden box
encasing this city's only water spigot.

Today's a no-water-day. No water until tomorrow,
maybe. Cement blocks, tar paper, corrugated sheets of tin.

A spray of bougainvillea. Penned pigs. Boys
pitching rocks at the neighbour's balding dog.

You approach an open door hoping for directions.
Inside, a greyhaired woman – grandchildren

wrapping themselves in her skirt – leans against a sink
filled with chipped dishes. A frayed piece of slip

used as a sling supports her arm.
She wants you to come in. Strung from a rafter,

one exposed light bulb. She waits for you
to sit on rusted bedsprings, offers a tortilla.

Stereo equipment heaped in a corner:
the kind you see at yard sales

and no one wants. Children everywhere.
A terrier and her puppies under the table.

Pigeons roaming the shadows, murmuring
small talk. The woman is speaking a language

you do not know but almost understand.
Above the table, a faded picture of the Last Supper.

A copper teakettle clock, wrapped in a plastic bag
to protect it from dust, tells the time.

Lines for the Kittiwakes

Too easy to accept the absence
of joy. And miss the most of it.

I hold on now to the way I lingered
over pages of a letter that crossed continents

and the way the scent of lilacs
surprised me through the open window

or the way the man polishing lighthouse lenses
paused in his work to pace the one circle possible,

enjoying the sound of his solemn voice
as he recited to me and the kittiwakes, *I was asleep*

but now I rise. Yes. Couldn't joy be waiting
just out of sight for the weary teacher

marking papers with precise red ticks,
for the mother in rehab missing her children,

or for the taxi driver on that slow, rainy night?
Somehow, isn't it woven into this fog-bound island

and into those long-ago street corners
where snow blurred sideways beneath the lights?

Somehow it exists. Somehow it wants to be found.

Rue de Lille

The same man who sang
in my dream, sings in the street
beneath my hotel room.

My first night in Paris, 4 a.m.,
and this man's a whole chorus –
not content to be just

a tenor, he takes all
the parts, one after another.
As he turns off rue de Lille

he's a soprano
heading towards the river.
Then a phrase of Brahms,

descending into baritone,
drifts back to my window –
Siehe, ich sage euch

ein Geheimnis. I know
these words, sang this Requiem
not long after my mother's death.

Behold I show you a mystery:
we shall not all sleep
but we shall all be changed...

There are times when it feels
we're lifted on something,
summoned by shadow, touch, or

some other element
we don't yet know. Like the brilliant
shades of a moth's wing

which depend upon emptiness.
Light strikes dark inner walls
and sends back trumpets of colour.

Wings iridescent as singing
that wakes you on a spring night.
Six years my mother's been gone

but it feels like a chorus of one.
Not quite asleep
but not quite changed.

The Throat Singers

With a half hour left before closing
and most of the museum still unexplored,
why was I unable to leave

the exhibit on Inuit throat singers?
I kept pushing the button
that played a film of two old women –

are they sisters? – standing nose-to-nose
in what looks like a musical duel.
As one lays down a challenge

with the sounds of muffled snow,
the other improvises riffs like ice
cracking. How deep their voices are,

probing a place far lower than expected.
It's as if by descending
they can sing from the inside of things.

They sing the metal rod used to chip through ice.
They sing water welling up through the hole.
They sing the wind, the sled, the dogs.

And from somewhere at the back of their throats,
known from a time before their births, they sing fire
to guide the hunters safely home.

Each woman holds the other's gaze. Shoulders
rise and fall together, as they play
a game where everything in their world's at stake.

Now at night, after watching that film so many times,
I seem to hear, right on the edge of my understanding,
the singing of old women

dressed in the flowered clothes of schoolgirls.
I think they're singing the silver fish scooped
from a hole, as well as the crackling plastic bag

they use to carry those fish. They name
the tilt of telephone poles and the sound
of grass pushing up through snow,

and the wind, also, swirling through that grass.
I'm going to sleep to the snowmobile's whine,
to the rattle of the prefab home's aluminium door

and the electric can opener's miracle drone.
My prayers hum as the women sing to young girls
who've come to learn their song.

They weave in the girls' names –
Winnie and Sarah. Somehow I'm hearing
the names of my children, too.

Their voices hold the stars of an Arctic sky.
The aurora borealis
on a baby's cap. They hold the baby itself

as it's tucked into fold after fold of sleep.
I give myself to the sounds of voices
singing from the insides of things.